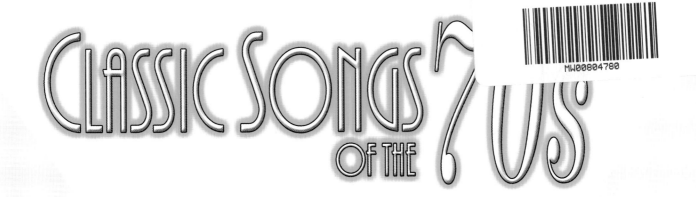

Project Manager: Carol Cuellar

Text By: Fucini Productions, Inc.

Cover Design: Joseph Klucar

Art Layout: Martha L. Ramirez

Production Coordinator: Donna Salzburg

CONTENTS

INTRODUCTION

People who know the '70s only as a time of pet rocks, mood rings, platform shoes, and polyester princes are getting just a small part of the story behind this memorable decade. The '70s were much more than goofy fads and gaudy fashions. In the ten years that separated the hippies of the '60s from the yuppies of the '80s, America went through one of the most pivotal periods in its history.

It was during the '70s that the counterculture of the '60s collided with the "Leave It to Beaver" sensibilities of mainstream America, changing both forever. The hippie movement disappeared amid the bright disco lights and smiley-face buttons of the '70s, but so too did many of the time-honored notions that middle America had about itself and the world.

How much did the '70s reshape American culture? We can get an idea by looking at some of the now-common phrases that entered our everyday vocabulary during this eventful decade: *energy crisis, Watergate, OPEC, organic, transcendental meditation, Earth Day, earthtones, disposable razors, personal newspaper ads, acupuncture, self-help books, health food, light beer, television miniseries, talk radio,* and *lifestyle,* to name a few.

So many features of daily life today can be traced back to the '70s. For instance, take the casual dress code found at most contemporary workplaces—it grew out of the leisure-suit and designer-jean trends of the '70s. Cell phones, which are so common today, are the successors to the '70s CB radio craze.

Many men started to get their hair "done" by a stylist rather than cut by a barber during the '70s, while women began breaking through barriers in the workplace, becoming everything from construction workers to big-city mayors. It was during the '70s that the landmark Equal Rights Amendment was passed, *Ms.* magazine was first published, and Billie Jean King bested Bobby Riggs in the celebrated "Battle of the Sexes" tennis match.

Americans were forced to confront the limitations of their own power in the '70s. The nation's troops were withdrawn from Vietnam, people waited in long lines at gas stations during the OPEC oil embargo, and odd-looking little cars from Japan threatened Detroit's dominance of the automobile industry.

The realization that life in the United States could be affected by other countries opened American's eyes to outside cultures. At the beginning of the '70s, few Americans had ever heard of, much less sampled, burritos, Szechuan food, or quiche. By the time the '70s drew to a close, such exotic fare would be common even in small towns.

Americans also broadened their taste in music in the '70s. Artists like Lynyrd Skynyrd ("Sweet Home Alabama") and the Charlie Daniels Band ("The Devil Went Down to Georgia") forged a raw style of Southern rock. Meanwhile, Barry Manilow ("Can't Smile Without You") and other artists were reviving the pop scene with mellow ballads that were a throwback to an earlier era.

The profound changes that reshaped America during the '70s also created a sense of unease in the country. In a decade that saw runaway inflation, a major accident at a nuclear power plant, and the resignation of a President of the United States, many Americans turned to music as a form of escape. They found it in the pulsating beats of the new disco music, as well as in some of the best storytelling ballads of all time.

So join us on this musical tour of the '70s. Whether your tastes run toward the mellowness of Kenny Loggins or the sultry beat of Donna Summer, you're sure to see why this decade ranks as one of the most memorable in the history of popular music. Oh . . . and have a nice day!

Rock Rolls On

Rock 'n' roll turned 20 in the '70s without losing the youthful exuberance that characterized its first two decades. The teenagers who came of age listening to Elvis Presley and Buddy Holly in the '50s were all grown-up now and busy raising teens of their own.

These aging members of the James Dean generation still listened to rock 'n' roll in the '70s, just as their children did. Sure, parents and children didn't always share the same tastes in rock artists or songs, but for the first time in the twentieth century, they both felt at home with the same kind of music.

Rock music not only bridged the generation gap in the '70s, but it also flowered in a variety of different new directions. Groups like Steely Dan (the duo of Donald Fagen and Walter Becker) mixed elements of jazz and blues to create a progressive-rock sound that appealed to listeners on a cerebral, as well as emotional, level. Steely Dan's collective talents are showcased in "Rikki Don't Lose That Number," a subtly ironic and neatly compact song that reached No. 3 on the charts. The Kinks also introduced a level of irony to rock with the 1970 hit "Lola."

Carlos Santana popularized a new psychedelic-tinged Latin-influenced rock in the early '70s with smash hits like "Evil Ways." The Mexican-born Santana formed his namesake group in San Francisco in the mid-'60s. Over the next five years, the group developed one of the most recognizable sounds in the history of rock music by blending 12-bar blues and driving rhythms with a blazing lead guitar. Santana's distinctive guitar solos, with their long sustained notes, lit up the rock scene in the '70s and provided a sensuous living link to the great guitarists of the '60s like Jimi Hendrix.

Other artists of the '70s were mixing hip '60s-style lyrics and rhythms with a traditional Nashville sound to create a new hybrid form of music that was a cross between rock and country. With her crystal-clear voice and flawless diction, Linda Ronstadt introduced millions to this new country-rock style in songs like "Blue Bayou." In 1974, Tennessee songwriter/performer Dave Loggins (cousin of superstar Kenny Loggins) released one of the most beautiful and enduringly popular country-rock hits, "Please Come to Boston." The song, which tells the story of a wandering young man and his patient girlfriend back in Tennessee, earned Loggins a Grammy and reached No. 5 on the pop charts while becoming an anthem for many restless youths of the '70s.

Gerry Beckley, Dewey Bunnell, and Dan Peek were sons of U.S. Air Force officers living in England when they formed the group America. Taking '60s-style psychedelic themes and giving them a folk-rock twist, the trio became wildly popular with fans of all ages on both sides of the Atlantic. Their haunting 1972 hit "A Horse With No Name" reached the top of the charts and helped earn them a Grammy as Best New Artist.

Another Best New Artist Grammy-winner of the early '70s was Carly Simon. With rock ballads like "That's the Way I've Always Heard It Should Be" and "You're So Vain," Simon gave voice to the wariness and frustration that many women felt about the sexual politics of life in the '70s. Though her vocal style had a soft, almost willowy quality to it, she also projected an image of self-assured determination. Unlike female vocalists of an earlier era, Simon approached the issue of romance from an entirely female perspective. Her songs were not about pleasing (or keeping) your man or recapturing lost romance, but about controlling your own destiny despite the vagaries of love. In so doing, they were early harbingers of a new era for women.

THE SECOND BRITISH INVASION

The British Invasion that reshaped popular music in America didn't end in the '60s. Years after Americans first met the Beatles, Rolling Stones, Animals, and other British groups, England unleashed another wave of musical innovation on her former colonies. The '70s were the breakout decade for three of the most popular British musical geniuses of all time: Eric Clapton, Rod Stewart, and Elton John.

Although all three artists had been playing professionally in the previous decade, it was in the '70s that they each achieved international acclaim as solo performers. In his own way, each of these gifted artists left an impact on rock that was still very much in evidence at the close of the twentieth century.

Eric Clapton was already established as a blues and rock guitar genius from his work with the Yardbirds, Bluesbreakers, and Cream when the '70s dawned, but the reticent musician from Surrey, England, had never enjoyed a solo career. This changed in August 1970 when he released the self-titled album, *Eric Clapton,* which featured the Top 40 hit "After Midnight."

Showcasing Clapton's raw power as a guitarist and his evocative vocals, the song became one of the most widely recognized and frequently played hits of the year. After a brief hiatus, Clapton returned to reel off a string of critically acclaimed hits in the mid-'70s, making him one of the few British artists to enjoy spectacular success as both the member of a band and a solo performer.

Like Clapton, Roderick (Rod) Stewart had tasted success in a band before reaching international superstardom as a solo artist. Stewart sang with the Jeff Beck Group briefly in the '60s and later performed with Faces, a rock band that included future Rolling Stones member Ron Wood. However, it's doubtful that Stewart would have become one of rock's most famous names had he not broken through as a solo artist.

In the summer of 1971, Stewart released his breakthrough solo album, *Every Picture Tells a Story,* which featured his No. 1 single "Maggie May." This song about a young man's romantic involvement with an older woman took on a poignant quality thanks to the intonations of Stewart's raspy world-weary voice and the haunting blend of acoustic guitar and organ sounds in the background. Like the conflicted feelings of its main character, "Maggie May" seemed timeless; its mandolin sound evoked images of a distant past, yet the lyrics, as performed by Stewart, sounded very contemporary. The song stayed on top of the charts for five weeks. At one point in September, the single and its album were both No. 1 in the U.S. and the U.K.

Elton John also enjoyed outstanding success on both sides of the Atlantic in the early '70s. A flamboyant singer/pianist with a penchant for outrageous clothes, high platform shoes, wild hair coloring, and onstage antics, John fit in perfectly with the decade's well-documented zany side. However, as music critics throughout the world quickly recognized, he was also an artist of uncompromising genius.

At times, John could pound the piano with the fiery passion of Jerry Lee Lewis or Little Richard. In other songs, like "Daniel," he revealed a softer side of his musical personality, conveying a sweet emotional yearning without being overly sentimental. In other songs, like the 1974 hit "Don't Let the Sun Go Down on Me," John showed yet another dimension of his talent by adding a subtle, but moving, bluesy feeling to his music.

John's best-known hit from the '70s is the poignant tribute to the tragic life and death of Marilyn Monroe, "Candle in the Wind." Written 12 years after the legendary film star's death, this song demonstrated that John's genius as a poet was equal to his talent on the keyboard. In 1997, John rewrote the song as a tribute to be performed at the funeral of his friend Princess Diana. The reworded song, released as "Candle in the Wind," became the most popular single of all time, outselling Bing Crosby's "White Christmas." Proceeds from the sale of this recording went to a memorial fund established in the princess's name.

Disco Divas and Dancing Queens

Studio 54 . . . *Saturday Night Fever* . . . mirror balls . . . strobe lights. For many people, the mere mention of the '70s conjures up instant images of disco dancing. With good reason—for much of the decade, it seemed like every big-city neighborhood and suburban shopping center had a club where you could spend the night gyrating on the dance floor to the synchronized beat of the new disco sound.

The glitz and glamour of disco music and dancing provided a perfect escape for Americans who were weary of waiting in long lines at the gas station and tired of scrimping on groceries to ward off the effects of inflation.

Disco also got rock music fans dancing again. After the twist and mashed potato years of the early '60s, dancing faded into the background of the rock scene. This all changed with the rise of the disco club in the '70s. Dancing was back—and it would remain a part of the rock experience for the rest of the twentieth century, even after the initial disco craze subsided.

No one embodied the image of the disco diva in the '70s as elegantly or as beautifully as Donna Summer. The sultry songstress from Boston captivated the music world with her brilliant blend of funk and sophistication. Dominating the disco scene, she won two Grammy Awards in the '70s and became the first female artist in history to have three No. 1 solo singles in one year.

Summer's breakthrough came in 1975 with the release of her steamy single "Love to Love You, Baby." First released in Europe, where it became a major hit, the song was edited to a shorter length for its American debut. It reached No. 2 on the Billboard Hot 100 in the U.S.

The success of "Love to Love You Baby" quickly established Summer and the entire disco genre as forces to be reckoned with in popular music. In future hits, like the No. 1 "MacArthur Park," a sizzling remake of a '60s classic, she demonstrated the vocal range and dramatic flair that gave her music an enduring value that transcended the disco era.

Other superstars of the '70s infused their pop songs with a disco beat and flavor. The Swedish group Abba was among the best at creating this attractive musical mix. In August 1976, the group celebrated the disco trend with the release of "Dancing Queen," its only No. 1 hit in the U.S. It is virtually impossible to listen to "Dancing Queen" without tapping your feet or having the song's catchy melody run through your head.

Like many Abba songs, including their 1974 breakout hit "Waterloo" and "S.O.S." (1975), "Dancing Queen" is a powerfully produced and expertly crafted song with perfect counterharmonies and irresistible arrangements. In 1977, Abba added a new, more graceful and textured dimension to their music with the hit "Knowing Me, Knowing You," which reached the top of the charts in the U.K. Growing into their distinctive sound, Abba helped define the pop music of the '70s and beyond.

Great Storytellers

When they weren't out on the disco dance floor, people could escape the pressures of daily life in the '70s by being swept up in one of the decade's great storytelling songs. Offering more than good music, these songs wove tales and painted pictures that transported listeners to another world. Narrative literary songs have been with us since the days of the ancient troubadours, but seldom has the art of musical storytelling reached the heights that it did in the '70s.

Many of the best story songs were inspired by the popular trends of the decade. This was true of "Escape (The Piña Colada Song)" by Rupert Holmes, which drew on two '70s trends: the newspaper personal pages and the piña colada beverage. Holmes' 1979 song about a couple's crossed signals reached No. 1 on the charts.

Other storytelling hits, like "The Devil Went Down to Georgia" by the Charlie Daniels Band, delved into the realm of fantasy. Inspired by a Stephen Vincent Benet poem, this song about a young man outplaying the devil to win a gold fiddle reached No. 1 on the country charts and No. 3 on the pop charts. It also introduced many Americans to the talented Daniels, who had been a highly regarded session player for years, recording with everyone from Bob Dylan to Hank Williams Jr.

Don McLean was among the most celebrated and gifted of the '70s balladeers. Born in suburban New Rochelle, New York, McLean wrote the musical biography of an entire generation with his No. 1 hit "American Pie." Released in the fall of 1971, this song quickly rose to the top of the charts, selling more than eight million copies as a single and an album.

An ode to the life and times of the first rock 'n' rollers, "American Pie" flowed from deep within its author's own experience. Words and music move effortlessly together in this masterpiece, weaving a rich tapestry of shared memories.

McLean's lyrics are wrought with deep meaning yet always open to interpretation. What exactly was revealed the "day the music died"? Is this a song that mourns the loss of youth and innocence? A requiem for rock 'n' roll itself? Or is it a celebration of a magical moment in popular music that challenges us to hope, dream, and believe that "music can save your mortal soul."

Perhaps both messages exist side by side in the complexity of "American Pie," leaving us to emphasize whichever one we choose. In any event, it is fitting that Don McLean wrote his masterpiece about the past and future of rock 'n' roll in the '70s, a decade when one era of our popular culture ended and another began.

THINGS THAT FIRST APPEARED IN THE '70S

1. Designer jeans
2. Personal computers
3. Child-proof bottles
4. Snowmobiles
5. Word processors
6. Floppy disks
7. Miller Lite beer
8. Disposable razors
9. VCRs (video cassette recorders)
10. Artificial hearts
11. Laser printers
12. Soft drinks in plastic bottles

AFTER MIDNIGHT

Words and Music by
JOHN J. CALE

After Midnight - 3 - 1

mid - night,___ we're gon - na chug-a-lug___ and shout. _____
mid - night,___ it's all gon - na be peach - es___ and cream. _____

We're gon - na stim-u-late___ some
We're gon - na cause talk and___ sus-

ac - tion;___ we're gon - na get some sat-is-fac-tion. We're gon-na find out
pi - cion;___ we're gon - na give an ex-hi-bi-tion. We're gon-na find out

what it is all a - bout._____
what it is all a - bout._____

After midnight,___ we're gon - na let it all___ hang

down.___

Repeat and fade

After mid - night,___ we're gon - na let it all___ hang

Repeat and fade

down.___

ALL BY MYSELF

Words and Music by
ERIC CARMEN and
SERGEI RACHMANINOFF

Lyrics:
When I was young___ I nev-er need-ed an-y-one,
Liv-in' a-lone, ___ I think of all the friends___ I've known,

and mak-in' love was just___ for fun; those days___ are gone.
but when I dial the tel-e-phone no-bod-y's home.

All by___ my-self, _____ don't wan-na be

AMERICAN PIE

Words and Music by
DON McLEAN

16

Em

This - 'll be the day ___ that I ___ die. ___

D7

G **Am**

1. Did you ___ write the book of love ___ and do you ___
2.-4. *See additional lyrics*

C **Am** **Em**

___ have faith in God a - bove? ___ If the Bi - ble tells ___

D **G** **D/F#**

___ you so ___ Now do you ___ be - lieve ___ in

Additional Lyrics

2. Now for ten years we've been on our own,
And moss grows fat on a rollin' stone
But that's not how it used to be
When the jester sang for the king and queen
In a coat he borrowed from James Dean
And a voice that came from you and me
Oh and while the king was looking down,
The jester stole his thorny crown
The courtroom was adjourned,
No verdict was returned
And while Lenin read a book on Marx
The quartet practiced in the park
And we sang dirges in the dark
The day the music died
We were singin'... bye-bye... etc.

3. Helter-skelter in the summer swelter
The birds flew off with a fallout shelter
Eight miles high and fallin' fast,
it landed foul on the grass
The players tried for a forward pass,
With the jester on the sidelines in a cast
Now the half-time air was sweet perfume
While the sergeants played a marching tune
We all got up to dance
But we never got the chance
'Cause the players tried to take the field,
The marching band refused to yield
Do you recall what was revealed
The day the music died
We started singin'... bye-bye... etc.

4. And there we were all in one place,
A generation lost in space
With no time left to start again
So come on, Jack be nimble, Jack be quick,
Jack Flash sat on a candlestick
'Cause fire is the devil's only friend
And as I watched him on the stage
My hands were clenched in fists of rage
No angel born in hell
Could break that Satan's spell
And as the flames climbed high into the night
To light the sacrificial rite
I saw Satan laughing with delight
The day the music died
He was singin'... bye-bye... etc.

ANTICIPATION

Words and Music by
CARLY SIMON

We _____ can nev-er know _____ a-bout the days _____ to come, _____ but _____ we think _____ a-bout them _____ an-y-

tell you _____ how eas-y _____ it feels to be _____ with you; _____ how right _____ your arms _____ feel _____ a-round

mor-row _____ we might not be _____ to-geth-er, _____ I'm no proph-et _____ and I don't _____ know na-ture's _____

an - tic - i - pa - tion __ is mak-ing me late, __

is keep-ing me wait - ing. And __

I - ing. And __ to -

these are the good old days. __ These are the good old days. __ And

stay right _ here, _ 'cause these are the good old days. _ These are the

good old days. _ These are the good old days. _

These are the good old days. _ These are _____

_ the good old days. _____

no chord

a tempo

AND I LOVE YOU SO

Words and Music by
DON McLEAN

BLUE BAYOU

Words and Music by
ROY ORBISON and
JOE MELSON

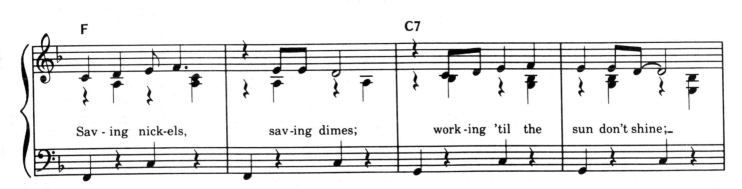

Blue Bayou - 3 - 1

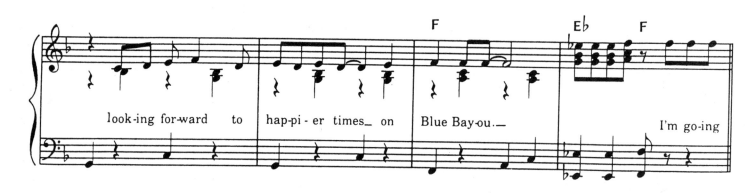

looking forward to happier times_ on Blue Bayou._ I'm going

Chorus:

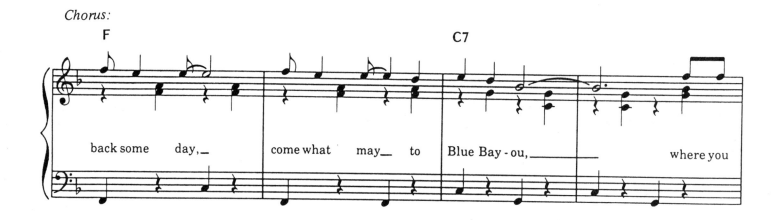

back some day,_ come what may_ to Blue Bay-ou,_____ where you

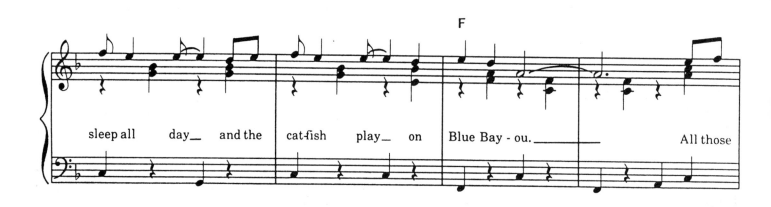

sleep all day_ and the cat-fish play_ on Blue Bay-ou._____ All those

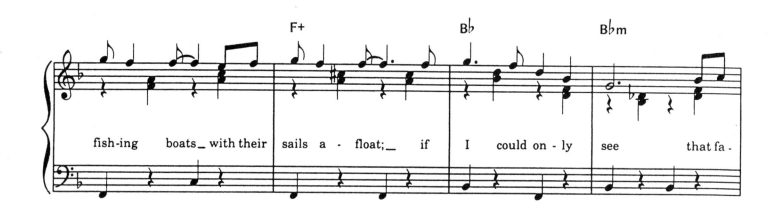

fish-ing boats_ with their sails a - float;_ if I could on - ly see that fa-

mil-iar sun-rise___ through | sleep-y eyes,___ how | hap-py I'd be.___

hurt-in' in-side.___ | I'll | nev-er be blue;___ my | dreams___ come true___

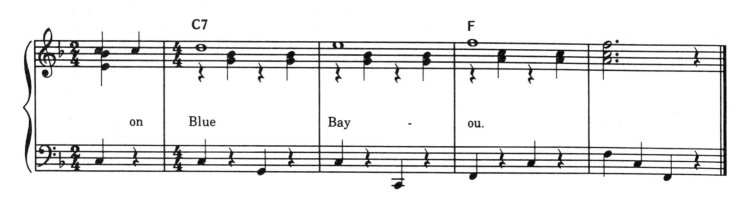

on | Blue | Bay - ou.

Verse 2:
Go to see my baby again
And to be with some of my friends;
Maybe I'd be happy then on Blue Bayou.
Saving nickels, saving dimes;
Working 'til the sun don't shine;
Looking forward to happier times on Blue Bayou.

Chorus 2:
I'm going back some day, gonna stay on Blue Bayou;
Where the folks are fine and the world is mine on Blue Bayou.
Ah, that girl of mine by my side, the silver moon and the evening tide,
Oh, some sweet day gonna take away this hurtin' inside.
I'll never be blue, my dreams come true
On Blue Bayou.

BAND OF GOLD

Words and Music by
RONALD DUNBAR and
EDITH WAYNE

BRANDY
(You're a Fine Girl)

Words and Music by
ELLIOT LURIE

Brandy - 3 - 1

Bran-dy used to watch his eyes _ when he told his sail-or's sto - ry, ___ She could

feel the o - cean fall and rise _ she saw its rag - ing glo - ry. ___ But

he had al - ways told ___ the truth, ___ Lord, he was an hon - est man; ___

Bran-dy does her best to un - der - stand. ___ At

CANDLE IN THE WIND

Words and Music by
ELTON JOHN and
BERNIE TAUPIN

42

46

CAN'T SMILE WITHOUT YOU

Words and Music by
CHRIS ARNOLD, DAVID MARTIN
and GEOFF MORROW

Can't Smile Without You - 4 - 1

DANIEL

Words and Music by
ELTON JOHN and
BERNIE TAUPIN

Moderately bright

1.4. Dan - iel is trav - 'ling to - night___ on a plane___
2. They say Spain is pret - ty 'though I've nev - er been ___
3. *Instrumental ad lib. at 1st D.S. (small notes)*

I can see the red ___ tail - lights ___
Well Dan - iel says ___ it's the best place ___ he's

Daniel - 4 - 1

54

Oh___ Dan-iel___ my broth-er___ you are old-er___ than me___ do you___ still feel the pain___ Of the scars___ that___ won't heal___ your eyes___ have___ died_____ But you see more___ than___ I___ Dan-iel you're a star In the face___ of the sky___

Daniel - 4 - 3

DANCING QUEEN

Words and Music by
BENNY ANDERSSON, STIG ANDERSON
and BJORN ULVAEUS

Strong rock

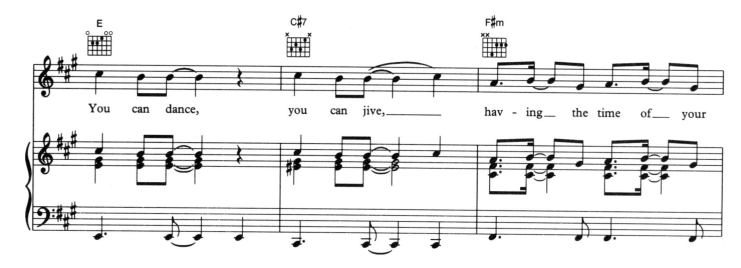

You can dance, you can jive,____ hav-ing__ the time of__ your

life.____ Oh,____ see that_ girl,__ watch that_ scene, dig in the

Dancing Queen - 5 - 4

THE DEVIL WENT DOWN TO GEORGIA

Words and Music by
CHARLIE DANIELS, JOHN THOMAS CRAIN, JR.,
WILLIAM JOEL DiGREGORIO, FRED LAROY EDWARDS,
CHARLES FRED HAYWARD and JAMES WAINWRIGHT MARSHALL

Fast Hoedown

The

The Devil Went Down to Georgia - 11 - 1

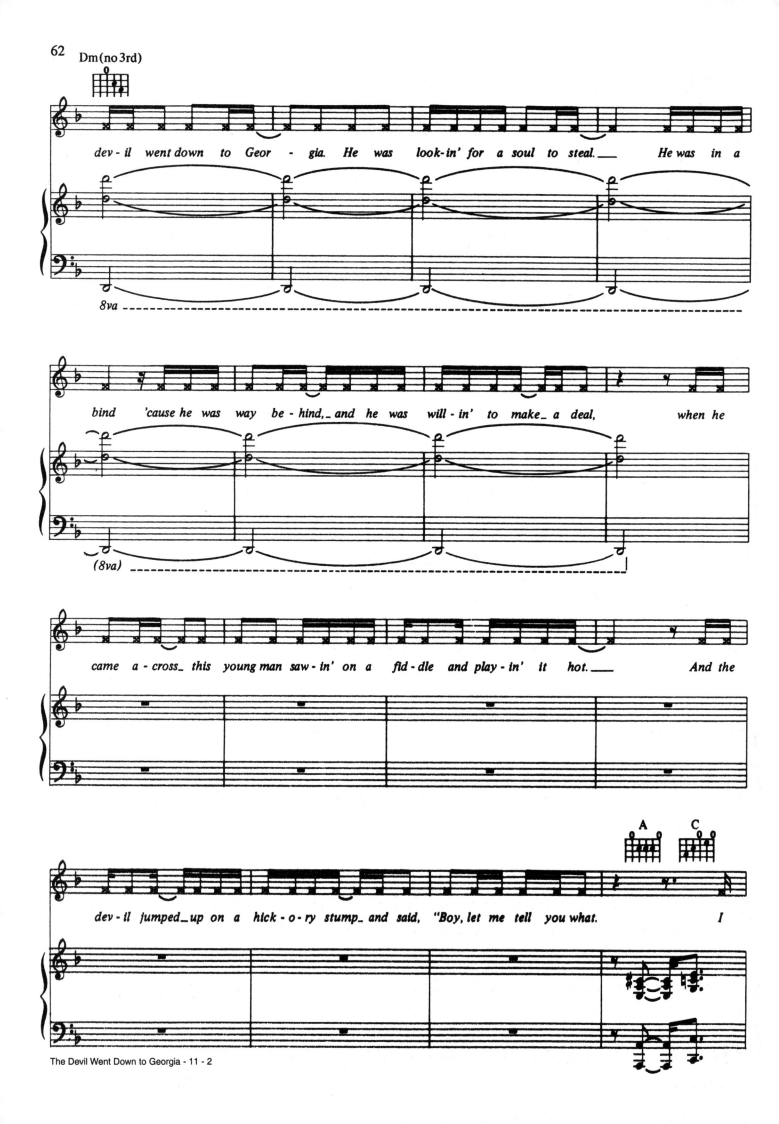

The Devil Went Down to Georgia - 11 - 4

if you win you get this shin-y fid-dle made of gold.   But

if you lose, the dev-il gets your soul. _____

The dev-il o-pened up his case and he

said, "I'll start this show." And fire____ flew from his fin - ger - tips as he

ros - ined up his bow.___ And he pulled the bow a - cross the strings and it made an e - vil

hiss. Then a band of de - mons joined in _ and it sound - ed some - thin' like this:

Gran - ny, does your dog bite? No, child, no.

He played,

DON'T LET THE SUN GO DOWN ON ME

Words and Music by
ELTON JOHN and
BERNIE TAUPIN

Don't Let the Sun Go Down on Me - 4 - 1

ESCAPE
(The Piña Colada Song)

Words and Music by
RUPERT HOLMES

Moderately

1. I was tired of my la - dy;
2. la - dy;

high hopes,

we'd been to - geth - er too long,___
I know that sounds kind of mean.___
and she walked in the place.___

like a worn - out re - cord a
But me and my old___ la -
I knew her smile in an in -

Escape - 5 - 1

there was this let - ter I read:____
I thought it was -n't half bad:____
and I said, "I nev - er knew____

"If you like pi - ña co-
"Yes, I like pi - ña co-
that you like pi - ña co-

la - das
la - das
la - das,

and get - ting caught in the rain,
and get - ting caught in the rain.
get - ting caught in the rain,

if you're not in - to yo - ga,
I'm not much in - to health food;
and the feel of the o - cean

if you have half a
I am in - to cham-
and the taste of cham-

EVIL WAYS

Words and Music by
SONNY HENRY

Evil Ways - 3 - 1

by. With Jean and Joan_ and a - who knows who.__ I'm get - tin'

tired__ of wait - in' and fool -in' a - round.__I'll find some - bod - y who won't make me

To Coda

feel like a clown.__This can't go on;_____ Lord_knows, you've got to

D.S. al Coda

change. When { I come { you

CODA

on;_____ Yea, yea, yea._____

GIVE ME JUST A LITTLE MORE TIME

Words and Music by
RONALD DUNBAR and
EDITH WAYNE

Give Me Just a Little More Time - 3 - 3

HEAVEN MUST BE MISSING AN ANGEL

Words and Music by
FREDERICK PERREN and
KENNETH St. LEWIS

Heav-en must be miss-ing an an - gel, ___ miss-ing an an - gel, child, ___ 'cause you're here with me right ___ now.

Your love is heav-en-ly, ba - by, ___

Heaven Must Be Missing an Angel - 5 - 1

Heaven Must Be Missing an Angel - 5 - 3

Heaven Must Be Missing an Angel - 5 - 5

HERE COMES THAT RAINY DAY FEELING AGAIN

Words and Music by
TONY MACAULAY, ROGER COOK
and ROGER GREENAWAY

1. -3. Here comes that rain - y day feel - ing a - gain
2. Here comes that rain - y day feel - ing a - gain

And soon love's tears will be fall - ing like rain
And I'll be dream - ing of you ba - by and then

It al - ways seems to be a Mon - day   Left o - ver mem
Your face is al - ways on my mind girl   I'm hop - ing soon

A HORSE WITH NO NAME

Words and Music by
DEWEY BUNNELL

A Horse With No Name - 5 - 1

96

A Horse With No Name - 5 - 2

WONDERFUL TONIGHT

Words and Music by
ERIC CLAPTON

Wonderful Tonight - 4 - 1

KNOWING ME, KNOWING YOU

Words and Music by
BENNY ANDERSSON, STIG ANDERSON
and BJORN ULVAEUS

Knowing Me, Knowing You - 4 - 1

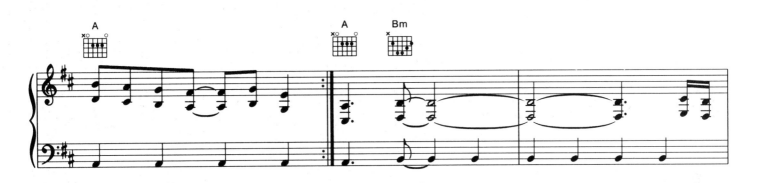

D.%. al Coda   ⊕ *CODA*

Know-ing me, know-ing   do.

repeat and fade

Knowing Me, Knowing You - 4 - 4

LOLA

By
RAY DAVIES

Slowly with a strong beat

met her in a club down in old So - ho __ where you drink cham-pagne and it tastes just like __ cher-ry
I'm not the world's most phy-si-cal guy, __ but when she squeezed me tight she near-ly broke my spine. __ oh my

co - la   C-O-L-A co - la.   She
Lo - la   la la __ la la Lo - la.   Well

walked up to me, and she asked me to dance _ I asked her her name and in a dark brown voice _ she said
I'm not dumb, but I can't un-der-stand _ why she walked like a wom-an and talked like a man oh my

Lo - la L-O-L-A Lo - la la la _ la la
Lo - la la la _ la la Lo - la la la _ la la

Lo - la.
Lo - la.

Well, Well, we

Lola - 6 - 2

that's the way_ that I want it to stay,_ and I____ al-ways want it to be that way_ for my

Lo - la la la_ la la Lo - la.

Girls will be boys, and boys_ will be girls, it's a mixed up, mud-dled up, shook up world_ ex-cept for

Lo - la la la_ la la Lo - la. Well,

LOVE TO LOVE YOU, BABY

Words and Music by
PETE BELLOTTE, GIORGIO MORODER
and DONNA SUMMER

Love to Love You, Baby - 3 - 1

love to love you, ba - by. I love to love you, ba - by.

F7-9 **Bbm** **Eb7-9** **Abmaj7** 4fr. **Dm7-5** **G7** *To Coda*

Do it to me a - gain and a - gain, you put me in such an aw - ful spin,_ in a spin.

Cm 3fr.

F7-9 **Bbm** **Eb7-9** **Abmaj7** 4fr.

116

MAGGIE MAY

Words and Music by
ROD STEWART and MARTIN QUITTENTON

Moderately bright

Wake up, Mag-gie, I think I got some-thing to say to you:___ It's

late Sep - tem-ber and I real - ly should be back at school. I

know I keep you a - mused,___ but I feel I'm be - ing used, Oh,

Maggie May - 3 - 1

Maggie May - 3 - 2

2. You lured me away from home, just to save you from being alone.
   You stole my soul, that's a pain I can do without.
   All I needed was a friend to lend a guiding hand.
   But you turned into a lover, and, Mother, what a lover! You wore me out.
   All you did was wreck my bed, and in the morning kick me in the head.
   Oh, Maggie, I couldn't have tried any more.

3. You lured me away from home, 'cause you didn't want to be alone.
   You stole my heart, I couldn't leave you if I tried.
   I suppose I could collect my books and get back to school.
   Or steal my Daddy's cue and make a living out of playing pool,
   Or find myself a rock and roll band that needs a helpin' hand,
   Oh, Maggie, I wish I'd never seen your face. (To Coda)

MacARTHUR PARK

Words and Music by
JIMMY WEBB

128

MacArthur Park - 10 - 9

NEVER MY LOVE

Words and Music by
DON and DICK ADDRISI

Never My Love - 2 - 1

MAMA TOLD ME (NOT TO COME)

Words and Music by
RANDY NEWMAN

134

PLEASE COME TO BOSTON

Words and Music by
DAVE LOGGINS

1. Please come to Bos - ton for the spring - time. I'm
2. Please come to Den - ver with the snow - fall. We'll

stay - ing here with some friends and they've got lots of room.
move up in - to the moun - tains so far that we can't be found and

You can sell your paint - ings on the side - walk, by a ca - fé where I
throw 'I love you' ech - o's down the can - yons. And then lie a - wake at

Please Come to Boston - 3 - 1

ADDITIONAL LYRICS

Verse 3.
    Please come to L.A. to live forever
    A California life alone is just too hard to build
    I live in a house that looks out over the ocean
    And there's some stars that fell from the sky
    Living up on the hill
    Please come to L.A., she just said no,
    Boy, won't you come home to me.
Repeat Chorus

REELIN' IN THE YEARS

Words and Music by
WALTER BECKER and
DONALD FAGEN

Moderately

Tacet

Your ev - er - last - in' sum - mer, you can see it fad - in' fast, so you
tell - in' me you're a gen - ius since you were sev - en - teen; in
spent a lot of mon - ey and I spent a lot of time; the

grab a piece of some - thin' that you think is gon - na last. Well, you
all the time I've known you I still don't know what you mean. The
trip we made to Hol - ly - wood is etched up - on my mind. Af - ter

C°/E♭   B°/D   A/C#   D

would-n't e-ven know a dia-mond if you held it in your hand; the
week - end at the col-lege did-n't turn out like you planned; the
all the things we've done and seen you find an-oth-er man; the

A/C#   Bm7   A

things you think are pre - cious I can't un - der - stand.
things that pass for know - ledge I can't un - der - stand.
things you think are use - less I can't un - der - stand.

Gmaj9

Are you reel-in' in the years,___ stow-in' a-way the

A   Gmaj9

time?___ Are you gath-er-in' up the tears,___

Reelin' in the Years - 3 - 2

RIGHT TIME OF THE NIGHT

Words and Music by
PETER McCANN

1.) Sun goes down ___ on a silk - y day;
2.) No use talk - ing when the sha - dows fall;

quar - ter moon walk - in' thru the Milk - y Way. ___ Oh, you and me ___ ba - by,
night birds call - ing and he says it all. ___

we could think of some - thin' to do. ___ It's the

Right Time of the Night - 3 - 1

REUNITED

Words and Music by
DINO FEKARIS and
FREDDIE PERREN

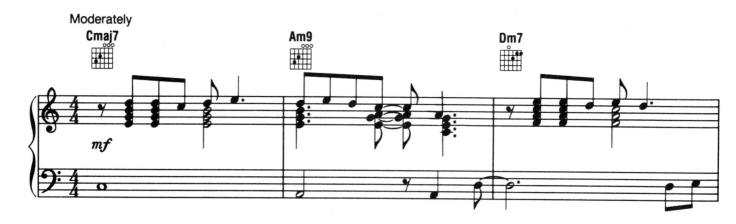

I was a fool to ev - er leave your side.___
I sat here star - ing at the same old wall.___

Me mi - nus you is such a lone - ly ride.___ The
Came back to life just when I got your call.___ I

Reunited - 4 - 1

3rd verse:

Lover, lover this is solid love,
  and you're exactly what I'm dreaming of.
All through the day and all through the night,
I'll give you all the love I have with all my might,
  hey, hey!

Lyric for Fade Ending:

Ooo, listen baby, I won't ever make you cry, I won't let one day go by
  without holding you, without kissing you, without loving you.
Ooo, you're my everything, only you know how to free
  all the love there is in me.
I wanna let you know, I won't let you go.
I wanna let you know, I won't let you go.
Ooo, feels so good!

RICH GIRL

Words and Music by
DARYL HALL

Rich Girl - 4 - 1

RIKKI DON'T LOSE THAT NUMBER

Words and Music by
WALTER BECKER and
DONALD FAGEN

Rikki Don't Lose That Number - 4 - 1

let - ter to your - self.

Rik-ki, don't lose that num - ber; it's the on - ly one you own.

You might use it if you feel bet - ter

when you get _____ home.

S.O.S.

Words and Music by
BENNY ANDERSSON, BJORN ULVAEUS
and STIG ANDERSON

Moderate steady four

Where are those hap - py days,___ they seem so hard___ to find?___
You seem so far___ a - way,___ though you are stand - ing near.___

I try to reach___ for you,___ but you have closed___ my mind.___
You make me feel___ a - live,___ but some - thing died___ I fear.___

S.O.S. - 4 - 1

D.%. al Coda

CODA

When you're gone,_____ how can I_____ ev-en try__ to go on?__
When you're gone,_____ though I try,_____ how can I__ car-ry on?__

slower

S.O.S. - 4 - 4

SORRY SEEMS TO BE THE HARDEST WORD

Words and Music by
ELTON JOHN and BERNIE TAUPIN

Sorry Seems to Be the Hardest Word - 4 - 1

It's sad ___ it's so sad ___ Why can't we talk it o - ver? ___ Al-ways seems to me ___ that
(it's so sad)

sor-ry seems to be ___ the hard - est word.

word. What do I do to make you love

SWEET HOME ALABAMA

Words and Music by
ED KING, RONNIE VAN ZANT and
GARY ROSSINGTON

Sweet Home Alabama - 5 - 1

I miss 'ole' 'bam - y once a - gain___ *(And I think it's a sin.)*

Verse

2. Well, I heard Mis - ter Young   sing a -

bout her.   Well, I heard ole Neil___ put her

down.   Well, I hope Neil Young   will re -

ADDITIONAL LYRICS

Verse 4.　Now Muscle Shoals has got the Swampers
　　　　　　And they've been known to pick a tune or two
　　　　　　Lord they get me off so much
　　　　　　They pick me up when I'm feeling blue
　　　　　　Now how about you.

Repeat Chorus and Fade

THAT'S THE WAY I'VE ALWAYS HEARD IT SHOULD BE

Words and Music by
CARLY SIMON and
JACOB BRACKMAN

That's the Way I've Always Heard It Should Be - 3 - 3

Additional Lyrics

2. My friends from college, they're all married now; they have their houses and their lawns.
   They have their silent noons, tearful nights, angry dawns.
   Their children hate them for the things they're not; they hate themselves for what they are;
   And yet they drink, they laugh, close the wounds, hide the scar.
   To Chorus:

3. You say that we can keep our love alive. Babe, all I know is what I see.
   The couples cling and claw and drown in love's debris.
   You say we'll soar like two birds thru the clouds, but soon you'll cage me on your shelf.
   I'll never learn to be just me first, by myself.
   To Chorus:

WATERLOO

Words and Music by
BENNY ANDERSSON, STIG ANDERSON and
BJORN ULVAEUS

Waterloo - 4 - 1

Waterloo - 4 - 4

THE WONDER OF YOU

Words and Music by
BAKER KNIGHT

1. When no - one else can un - der - stand me,
2. And when you smile, the world is bright - er.
3. You'll nev - er know how much I love you.

when ev - 'ry - thing I do is wrong, you give me love and con - so -
You touch my hand and I'm a king. Your kiss to me is worth a
My love is yours and yours a - lone, and it's so won - der - ful to

The Wonder of You - 2 - 1

HOUSE AT POOH CORNER

Words and Music by
KENNY LOGGINS

Chris-to-pher_ Rob - in and I_____walked a - long_ un-der branch-
Win - nie the Pooh does-n't know_ what to do, _ got a hon -

House at Pooh Corner - 5 - 1

VINCENT
(Starry, Starry Night)

Words and Music by
DON McLEAN

YEAR OF THE CAT

Words and Music by
IAN ALASTIR STEWART and
PETER WOOD

YOU'RE SO VAIN

Moderately

Words and Music by
CARLY SIMON

You walked in -
had me sev - er -
hear you

- to the par -
al years_
went up to Sar -

- ty
- a - go,
- a - to - ga,

like you were walk - ing on - to___ a
when I was still quite_ na -
and your horse nat - 'ral - ly

yacht.
ive.
won.

Your hat stra -
Well, you
Then you

te - gi - c'lly
said that we
flew your Lear

dipped be - low___ one
make such a pret - ty
jet up to No - va Sco - tia,___

eye,___
pair,___
to see the

your scarf, it was ap - ri -
and that you would nev - er
to - tal e - clipse___ of the

THE CLASSIC SONGS SERIES

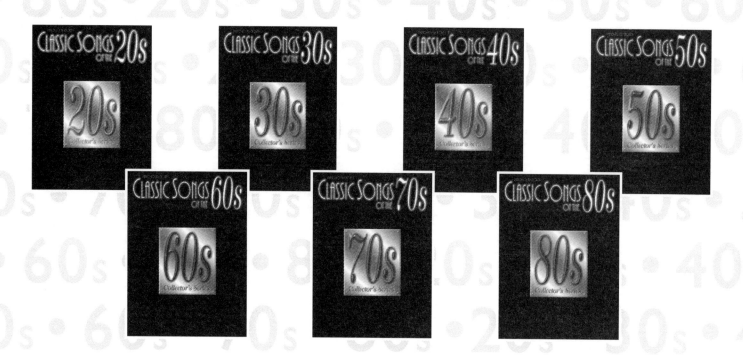

CLASSIC SONGS OF THE 20s
(MFM0111)

Titles include: **Ain't Misbehavin'** • **Charleston** • **Dinah** • **Do-Do-Do** • **Hallelujah!** • **I Know That You Know** • **I'll See You in My Dreams** • **Let's Do It** • **Mexicali Rose** • **My Man** • **Singin' in the Rain** • **Strike Up the Band** • **Sweet Georgia Brown** • **Tea for Two** • **Without a Song** • **You Do Something to Me** and many more!

CLASSIC SONGS OF THE 30s
(MFM0112)

Titles include: **A Foggy Day** • **Anything Goes** • **Blue Moon** • **Body and Soul** • **Caravan** • **I've Got You Under My Skin** • **Love Is Here to Stay** • **Moonlight Serenade** • **My Funny Valentine** • **Nice Work if You Can Get It** • **Over the Rainbow** • **Sophisticated Lady** • **Zing! Went the Strings of My Heart** and many more!

CLASSIC SONGS OF THE 40s
(MFM0113)

Titles include: **Boogie Woogie Bugle Boy** • **Come Rain or Come Shine** • **Don't Get Around Much Anymore** • **Fools Rush In** • **I Got It Bad (And That Ain't Good)** • **I've Got a Gal in Kalamazoo** • **Laura** • **'Round Midnight** • **Skylark** • **So in Love** • **'Tis Autumn** • **You'd Be So Nice to Come Home To** and many more!

CLASSIC SONGS OF THE 50s
(MFM0114)

Titles include: **Bird Dog** • **Good Golly Miss Molly** • **La Bamba** • **Let the Good Times Roll** • **Mack the Knife** • **Primrose Lane** • **Rock Around the Clock** • **Shake Rattle & Roll** • **Smoke Gets in Your Eyes** • **Splish Splash** • **Why Do Fools Fall in Love?** and many more!

CLASSIC SONGS OF THE 60s
(MFM0115)

Titles include: **The Birds and the Bees** • **Candy Man** • **Do You Know the Way to Dan Jose?** • **The House of the Rising Sun** • **I Got You Babe** • **I Say a Little Prayer** • **I Want to Hold Your Hand** • **The Lion Sleeps Tonight** • **Oh, Pretty Woman** • **Secret Agent Man** • **You Don't Own Me** and many more!

CLASSIC SONGS OF THE 70s
(MFM0116)

Titles include: **American Pie** • **Blue Bayou** • **Candle in the Wind** • **Dancing Queen** • **Heaven Must Be Missing an Angel** • **A Horse with No Name** • **Maggie May** • **The House at Pooh Corner** • **Rikki Don't Lose That Number** • **S.O.S** • **Sweet Home Alabama** • **Wonderful Night** • **You're So Vain** and many more!

CLASSIC SONGS OF THE 80s
(MFM0117)

Titles include: **Against the Wind** • **Back in the High Life Again** • **Crazy for You** • **Hard Habit to Break** • **Hotel California** • **Man in the Mirror** • **Rosanna** • **That's What Friends Are For** • **Tonight I Celebrate My Love** • **What's Love Got to Do with It** and many more!

All titles are Piano/Vocal/Chords

Printed in USA

AD0126 07/01